WHO'S THE CUTEST?
in 3-D

CONTENTS

Take a new look at some of nature's most adorable creatures, and find out just why they are so appealing. From fluffed up chicks to tiny furry friends, this book is full of facts about their lovable habits and some of their less appealing antics. Then you might be able to choose which ones you love the most!

KITTENS or PUPPIES

It's a never-ending argument and there is no easy answer. Do cats rule the roost, or are dogs REALLY a person's best friend? Prepare for battle...

CUTIE CATS

Kittens look adorable, with their button nose, pricked up ears, and dainty little paws. A cat will settle on your knee with a purr that warms your heart. Their padding feet knead and press into your lap as if you are the only person in the world. But then, a cat only comes for cuddles on its own terms, as they can be sniffy and aloof.

DARLING DOGS

Puppies are bright eyed bundles of love, and grow into adults that adore their owner. They love to lick to show how much they care, and their tails wag so hard that their whole body trembles. Bear in mind, though, that dogs can be smelly, loud, and need a lot of attention.

LIONS or TIGERS

Everyone knows that these creatures are two of the fiercest hunters around. But how can anyone resist the cutest cubs on the planet?

BABY CLOTHES
Lion cubs often have a spotted coat to help camouflage them. Their mother leaves them in the long grass while she hunts for food. She doesn't risk joining the rest of her group, or pride, until the cubs are two months old.

EARNING HIS STRIPES

Tiger cubs are feisty little things! At birth, they are blind and helpless, but by eight weeks old they are ready to learn how to hunt. They learn by following their mother and copying what she does.

TINY TERRORS

It might be impossible to choose between these tiny terrors. Both look like they were made in a cuddly toy factory! Big blue eyes make tiger cubs striking to look at, while lion cubs tumble and play together in the most adorable way.

ORANGUTANS or CHIMPS

The great apes, including chimpanzees and orangutans, are people's closest animal relatives. Just like us, their babies need their mothers to feed and look after them for many years.

HANGING AROUND
Orangutans are excellent climbers, even when they're tiny. If a baby's arms aren't long enough to reach, the mother acts as a bridge to help it across.

CHEEKY CHIMPS

Baby chimps have a pink face, and a tuft of white fur by their bottom. It helps other adults to see that they are still young and playful. They will forgive the babies for being annoying!

POOPER SCOOPERS
These bundles of fun aren't delightful all of the time. Orangutans eat their own poop, while chimpanzees pick it up and throw it around. Not so nice!

SQUIRRELS or CHIPMUNKS

Chipmunks are a type of squirrel, but they spend more time on the ground than red squirrels. They both use their tiny front paws to hold food as they nibble it daintily. Aw!

BOUNDING AROUND

Red squirrels can race up and down and around tree trunks faster than you can run in a straight line. In winter, their ears grow long tufts that stick far above their head.

CHEEKY CHAPPY

Chipmunks are very noisy, making chirruping sounds to attract their friends. They collect food in their cheek pouches to carry it home. Their cheeks can grow three times bigger when stuffed with food!

FAMOUS NAMES

Both creatures are bright eyed and bushy tailed and very, very cute. But chipmunks win the fame game hands-down, with Disney's Chip and Dale in cartoons, and Alvin and his chipmunk friends starring on the big screen.

Here's evidence that even the scariest creatures have their adorable side. Both these animals have big claws, enormous teeth, and small, lovable cubs!

SNOW BABIES

A newborn polar bear is tiny and its fur is so fine it looks almost bald. The cub grows really fast and is soon able to pad around on its oversized paws, poking its nose into everything around it. In the wild, they stay close to their mother until they are two years old.

CUTE CUBS

Bear cubs are playful and clumsy-looking, ambling and rolling around with their brothers and sisters. Small cubs learn how to climb trees, and seem to especially enjoy playing in puddles!

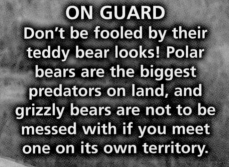

ON GUARD

Don't be fooled by their teddy bear looks! Polar bears are the biggest predators on land, and grizzly bears are not to be messed with if you meet one on its own territory.

EAGLES or OWLS

These beautiful birds of prey are both majestic hunters. Many people admire them despite their sharp beaks and claws. Their babies, on the other hand, will win hearts with their scruffy, fluffy cuteness.

REGAL EAGLE

Grown-up eagles have a gorgeous feather coat. Eagle chicks are not so well groomed! They are more like a bundle of fluff, with big eyes that are always on the lookout for food.

SILENT SWOOP

An owl's feathers are designed to make no noise at all as they fly. Baby owls have soft, short feathers and cannot fly when they are little. They explore by "branching" where they jump around on rocks and trees to make their legs and wings stronger.

NOT SO NICE

Cute they may be, but owls and eagles are birds of prey, and so they eat creatures. They gobble them whole, bones, claws and all, and then regurgitate (vomit up) the tough bits in a pellet.

CAMELS or KANGAROOS

Meet two desert dwellers that are each cute in their own way. Their survival tactics allow them to last for months at a time without drinking water. Cute AND amazing!

A BUMPY RIDE
Bactrian camels have two humps on their back, while the dromedary has only one. As adults, they are huge, sturdy beasts, but their babies are much softer and smaller.

NO GOING BACK
A kangaroo uses its strong tail and back legs for walking and jumping. But it can't hop backwards! The baby is called a joey and lives in a pouch on its mother's tummy for the first seven or eight months.

ELEPHANTS or RHINOS

Here's evidence that big mommas can have dinky, darling offspring! Elephants and rhinos are the two biggest creatures on land, making their babies look small and extremely cute in comparison.

ON THE RUN
An elephant calf takes time to get used to its long trunk. They swing it around wildly, and sometimes even trip over it or step on it! They also put it in their mouth and suck it, like a child sucks its thumb.

BABY FACE

Baby rhinos are born without a horn. It grows on the end of their nose when they are just a few weeks old. White rhinos have a very wide mouth that makes them look a little bit sad all the time.

WATCH OUT!

How do you decide between these two? Perhaps a good soaking from an elephant's trunk might put you off? Or a rhino on the run? Grown up rhinos charge at anything and everything, as they have such poor eyesight they don't know what is their enemy. They have even been known to attack rocks and trees!

SKUNKS or RACCOONS

Here are two animals that prove looks can be deceptive! Both look like adorable, angelic creatures, but both of them have hidden horrors!

KICKING UP A STINK
A tiny skunk takes after its parents, and can spray a disgusting smell from its rear end at the age of only one month. Don't get too close!

YARD RAIDERS

Rascally raccoons are often unwelcome, even though they look so sweet. They steal trash and leave a trail of destruction behind them. They also damage attics, chimneys, and other small spaces by setting up home there.

IN BLACK AND WHITE

That's the bad side to this pair, but just look at their cute little striped faces and bodies! Add to that their tiny little paws, twitchy nose, and bright button eyes, and they're hard to resist.

BEAVERS or OTTERS

These must be some of the most adorable water babies you will find. Beavers make their homes in rivers and lakes, while otters live in rivers or sometimes in the ocean.

BUSY BUILDERS
A beaver's huge front teeth allow it to chew through wood to build its lodge. Their large, flat tail acts like a paddle to steer as they swim.

STAYING AFLOAT

An otter has thicker fur than any other animal. The fur traps air to keep the otter warm. A baby otter's fur is so full of air that it can't actually dive under water!

YOU CHOOSE

Beavers and otters are both active, busy, even playful creatures. They squeal and call to each other. A beaver can make a sound like a crying child! Otters chirp, purr, and gurgle, and love to wrestle and slide down muddy banks into the water. How can you choose which is the cutest?!

ZEBRAS or GIRAFFES

Growing up on the dry plains of Africa is a tough start to life. A mother giraffe or zebra has to take great care of her vulnerable, adorable mini-me.

BABY STRIPES
A zebra foal's coat may have pale brown stripes so it can hide in the dry grass and stay safe. These stripes soon change to match its parents' markings.

TALL TODDLERS
Even at birth, giraffes are tall. A newborn is around 6 feet (the height of a grown man). They lie down for short naps and curl their neck to rest their head on their body.

WHO'S CUTEST?
Both these babies are adorable, but both can give you a mighty kick. In addition, a baby zebra has very large teeth! Giraffes have very tough mouths for shredding trees, and it makes them dribble and drool a lot.

RED DEER or REINDEER

Proud owners of magnificent antlers, these deer are found in snowy winter landscapes where their thick fur keeps them warm and dry.

HERE I AM!
Young red deer fawns make a high-pitched squeal to call their mother. They also bleat like lambs. Fully grown adult males roar and bellow to show off.

GROWING UP

Cute red deer fawns grow into graceful adults with beautiful red coats. Reindeer may start life as funny, fuzzy creatures with a bewildered look on their face, but they also mature into magnificent adults that are wonderful to watch.

WHERE ARE YOU, DEER?

Reindeer, also called caribou, travel in large herds. Their ankles make a clicking noise when they walk so they can keep track of each other, even when they can't see each other through the snow.

CHICKENS or DUCKS

Fluffy, baby birds are some of the cutest creatures around. With a waddle and a flap, they cheep and chirp their way into your heart. There's no denying, however, they leave their mark. You will be waddling yourself as you try to avoid stepping in bird mess!

BIRD BATH
Chicks can get clean by rolling in the dirt! Taking a dust bath gets rid of pesky biting bugs that live in their feathers.

CHEEKY CHICKS
Little chicks love to run and jump and sunbathe! They peck at grain and eat grass, slurping it into their beak like spaghetti!

DELIGHTFUL DUCKLINGS

A mother duck has lots of babies in one go. It is common for her to have at least ten ducklings following her around. Ducklings make a tiny chirping, peeping noise instead of a proper quack.

COMPLETELY QUACKERS

A duck's quack is its trademark call, and sounds just as though it is holding a conversation with you. (Ducks are quite clever, but not THAT clever!) They need to dip their head in water from time to time to keep their eyes wet, as ducks can't cry. Aw!

Here's a pair of creatures that don't like to be alone. Donkeys and goats get as sad as a person would if they are left on their own in a field all day.

GORGEOUS GOATS

Full-size goats grow taller than a child, but pygmy goats stay small and adorable their whole life. They are clever and fun-loving, head butting each other affectionately. They will make you laugh in the rain: they hate to get wet and will dance around puddles to avoid them!

DINKY DONKEYS

A donkey can be kind and gentle, and loves to play. They will run around in circles, carry balls and hoops, and have fun rolling in the dirt.

CUTE DESTROYERS!

If a donkey is bored, it will make a mess, chewing nearby fences, barns, and trees. As for goats: they always seem to be looking for mischief. They eat anything that looks edible (including the packet their food comes in) and climb everywhere. Goats climb on cars, on roofs, and even on you, and their hooves are sharp!

LAMBS or PIGLETS

Who can resist these crazy little creatures? They are two of the most adorable animals in the farmyard.

LOVELY LAMBS

Just look at the facial expressions on these woolly babies! Young lambs love to leap and explore and tumble in the fields with their brothers and sisters. They play chase and shout to each other in their shaky little voices. What's a sheep's worst characteristic? Probably the gas they produce from eating all of that grass!

PERKY PIGLETS

Tiny pigs are one of the most playful creatures you could wish to see. They love to have their own toys, and can play football! Then when they are worn out they will climb into bed and sleep on top of each other. Don't make them angry; some pigs have a reputation for being bad tempered.

FOALS or CALVES

Here's proof that big babies can be cute, too!
Which farm animals are your favorite?

PRECIOUS PONIES
Newborn foals are vulnerable and adorable, with their wobbly legs and fluffed up coat. Watch them as they struggle to their feet and begin to explore their surroundings within hours of being born. Be careful, though. A young pony might try to nibble you!

CUDDLY COWS

Calves have luscious long eyelashes and ears that look huge compared to their small, baby head. Their wet, shiny nose is perfect for nuzzling your hand in search of affection. Keep your toes away from their hooves, however, as even a small cow weighs as much as a fridge!

GUINEA PIGS or RABBITS

With bright eyes and a twitchy nose, who can choose between a rabbit and a guinea pig? Or maybe you don't have to, if you're allowed to keep one of each! Don't put them in the same hutch, however, as rabbits might bully their smaller room-mates.

GORGEOUS GUINEA PIGS

Have you ever seen a guinea pig beg for food? They stand on their back legs to attract your attention in the cutest way. They also love to run and jump when they are happy, and this activity has the best name; it is known as popcorning!

RABBIT HABITS

Rabbits can jump, and they can also dance! Their little leaps and turns are called binking. Of course, a rabbit's most famous assets are its twitchy nose and fluffy tail, not forgetting its wonderful, strokeable ears and fur.

BE WARNED!

Both rabbits and guinea pigs have some dirty little secrets, such as eating their own poop! They also scent mark their territory, but a rabbit's scent gland is under its chin, while a guinea pig has to drag its bottom along the floor.

CHEETAHS or LEOPARDS

These African cats may be related, but they are very different. The cheetah is a super speedy, slender hunter, while a leopard is big, strong, and powerful. Both have a gorgeous spotted coat for camouflage.

CRYING EYES

The tear marks under a cheetah's eyes help it to see better in the glaring sunshine. They don't mean that the cheetah is sad!

CHANGING ITS SPOTS

A leopard cub's fur is pale, fluffy, and has fainter spots than its parents. As it grows older the spots develop into distinctive rosettes with a pale middle and dark edges.

ON THE PROWL

These two cats hunt in different ways. A cheetah uses bursts of speed to chase its prey, but gets tired very quickly and gives up the chase. Leopards hunt at night, creeping up close and then pouncing out of the darkness. They are great at swimming and climbing, too. Which one would you be?

ELKS or GAZELLES

The gazelle is a member of the antelope family, while an elk is a type of deer. Antelopes grow horns and deer grow antlers, but both have spindly-legged babies with a lovable look.

SO SOFT
An adult male elk grows large antlers that are covered in a soft, furry velvet when they are new.

HIDE AND SEEK
The spots on an elk calf allow its mother to leave it hidden in long grass while she looks for food. The baby has no scent, so predators cannot sniff it out.

RUNNING AWAY
Gazelles are graceful creatures with beautiful faces and large eyes and ears. They are fast runners, and leap high in the air when they are chased in an action called "pronking."

COYOTES or FOXES

Members of the dog family, these clever creatures live in the wild but are both becoming a more common sight around towns and cities, searching for things to eat.

CUB COUNT
Coyote cubs or pups are born in litters of between five and seven. They walk on tiptoe to move silently.

DADDY'S HOME

A mother fox looks after her babies in their den, as they are totally helpless when they are born. The father goes out hunting to bring back food for them all.

WILD THINGS

These adorable animals may look like dogs, but they are wild creatures. A mother will protect her pups if you try to get too close.

KOALAS or PANDAS

These two tree dwellers live in very different places, but have remarkably similar habits. Both spend nearly their whole life sleeping or eating, and much of it perched up a tree!

KOALA CUDDLES
Baby koalas are tiny at first, and spend their whole time inside a pouch on their mother's tummy. Eventually, they climb out and cling on for dear life, riding piggyback until they are too big and heavy to be carried. Koalas can snooze for 18 hours a day!

PINK PANDA

When a panda is born it is blind and pink-skinned and only as long as a pencil. After a week, black patches appear on its skin, and by a few weeks old it has black and white fur. Before long, it will be running, rolling, and playing hide and seek.

YUCK!

What could possibly put you off creatures that look as cuddly as this? This might: the babies of both species eat their mother's poop. That's not cute!

SEALS or PENGUINS

When conditions get cold, creatures get cuddly! Bundles of fluff, they are well protected from icy waters and biting winds.

SEALED WITH A KISS
Seal babies are called pups. Seals usually have one pup per year, and it has to stay on land until it is covered in waterproof fur instead of its baby fluff.

SUPER SWIMMERS

Penguins can't fly, but that somehow makes them more appealing. Their little legs and flippered feet give them an adorable waddle instead of a walk. Their chicks look like something straight out of a toy store!

SOMETHING FISHY

If this book was scratch and sniff, you would quickly realize there's a non-cute side to these animals. Penguins and seals can be pretty stinky. Both are very loud, too, so you won't know whether to cover your ears or hold your nose!

WHO IS THE WINNER?

Take a look at this line up of every adorable creature that you've read about. It's enough to make you feel warm and squishy inside!

KITTENS PUPPIES

LIONS TIGERS

ORANGUTANS CHIMPS

SQUIRRELS CHIPMUNKS

POLAR BEAR BEARS

EAGLES OWLS

CAMELS KANGAROOS

ELEPHANTS RHINOS

SKUNKS RACOONS

BEAVERS OTTERS

ZEBRAS GIRAFFES